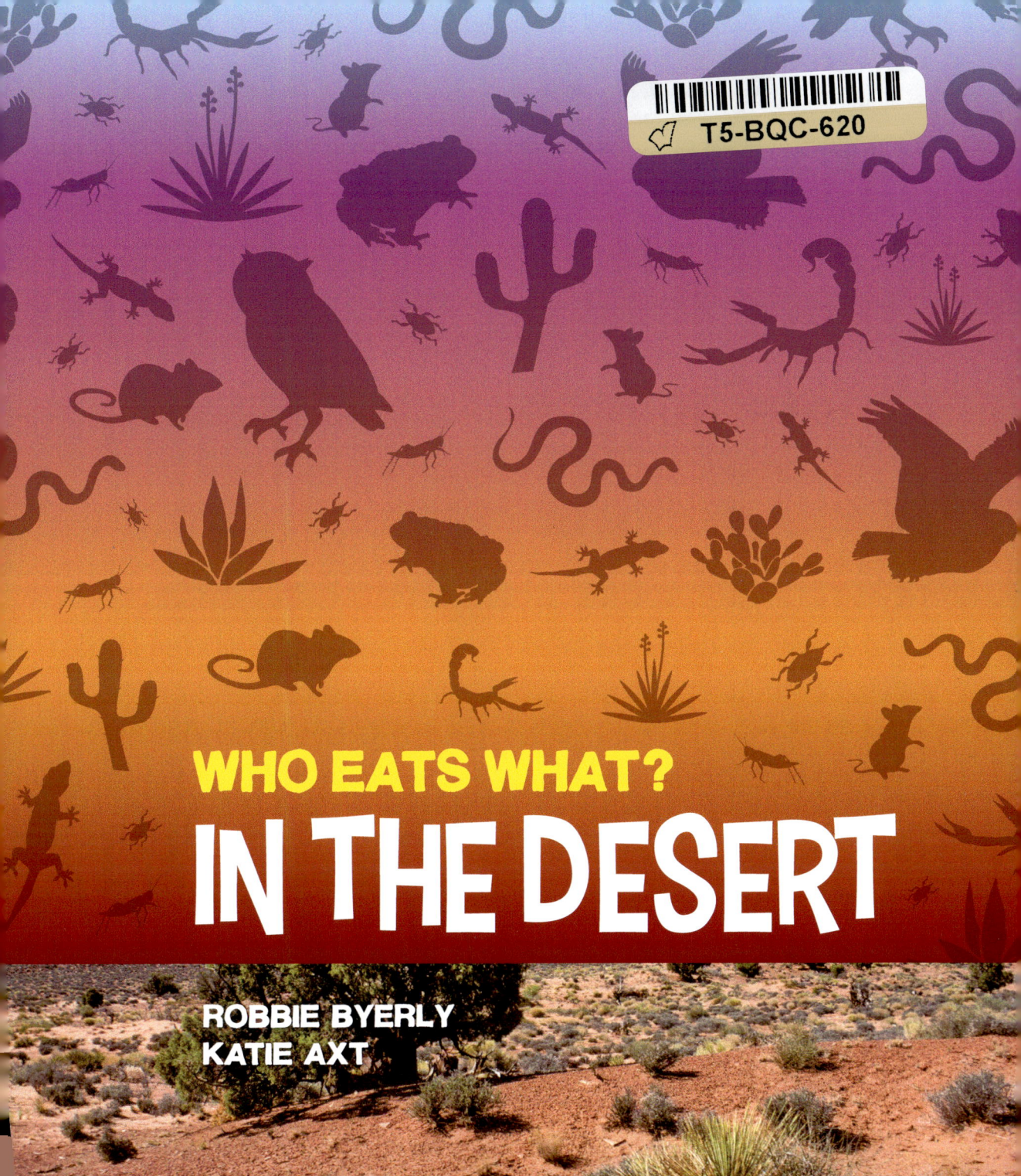

WHO EATS WHAT?
IN THE DESERT

ROBBIE BYERLY
KATIE AXT

This is a desert.

There are plants in the desert.

There are animals in the desert.

The animals have to eat to live.

Who eats what?

This is a plant.

The little bug eats the plant.

The big bug eats the little bug.

The lizard eats the big bug.

toad

mouse

snake

Who eats the lizard?

The snake eats the lizard.

This is a plant.

The mouse eats the plant.

The lizard eats the mouse.

The snake eats the lizard.

bug

owl

toad

Who eats the snake?

17

The owl eats the snake.

This is a plant.

The bug eats the plant.

The toad eats the bug.

The snake eats the toad.

The owl eats the snake.

The owl eats lots of animals.

Who eats the owl?

No one eats the owl.

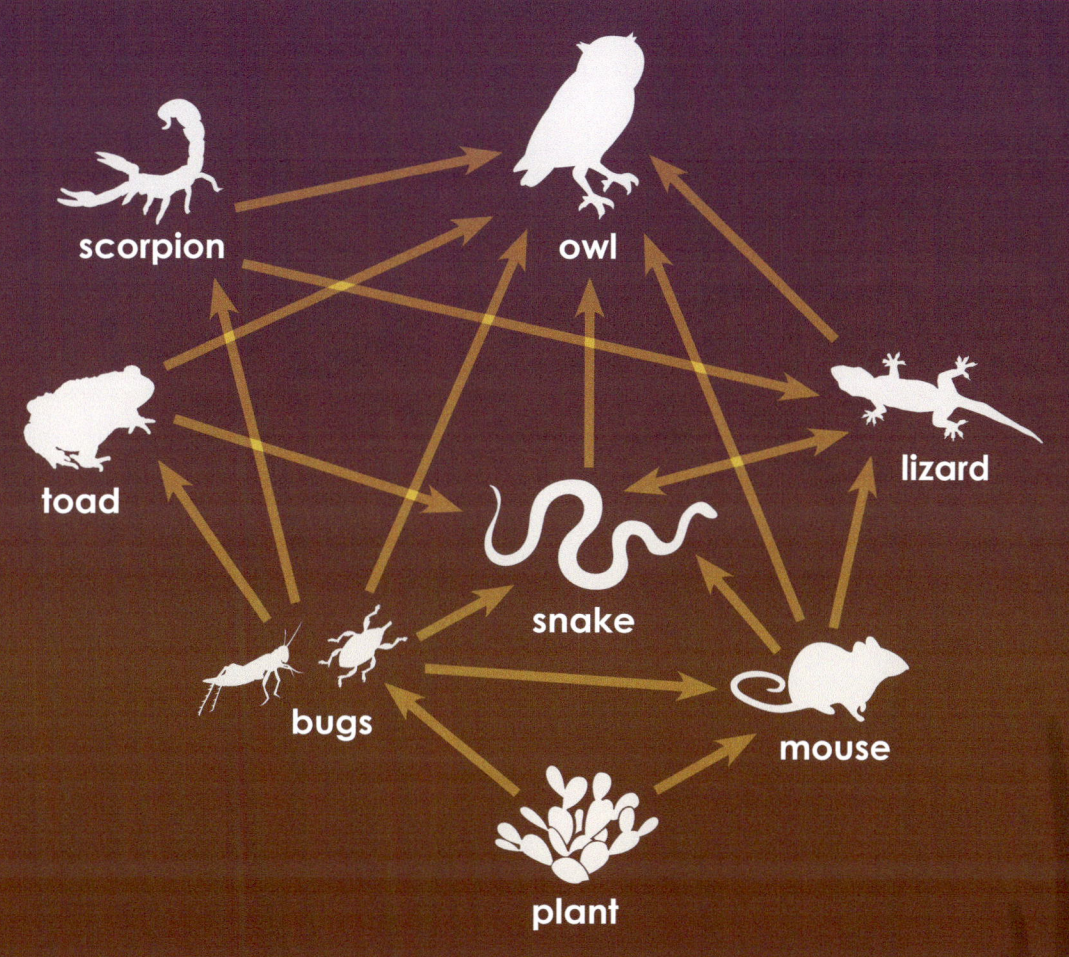

DESERT FACTS

 **Plants** in the desert include many types of cacti, agave plants, yucca plants, short grasses, bushes, and flowers.

 **Bugs**, such as the grasshopper, eat plant leaves, flowers, seeds, and fruit.

 **Toads** eat bugs such as ants, grasshoppers, beetles, and spiders.

 **Scorpions** eat other bugs and are also known to eat small animals, birds, and other scorpions.

 **Lizards**, such as the collared lizard, eat bugs, plants, small animals, and other lizards.

 **Snakes** eat small animals like toads, mice, birds, lizards, and bugs.

 **Mice** eat plants, fruit, seeds, and small bugs.

 **Owls**, such as the great horned owl, are great hunters and eat bugs, birds, lizards, snakes, rabbits, mice, toads, armadillos, and other animals in the desert.